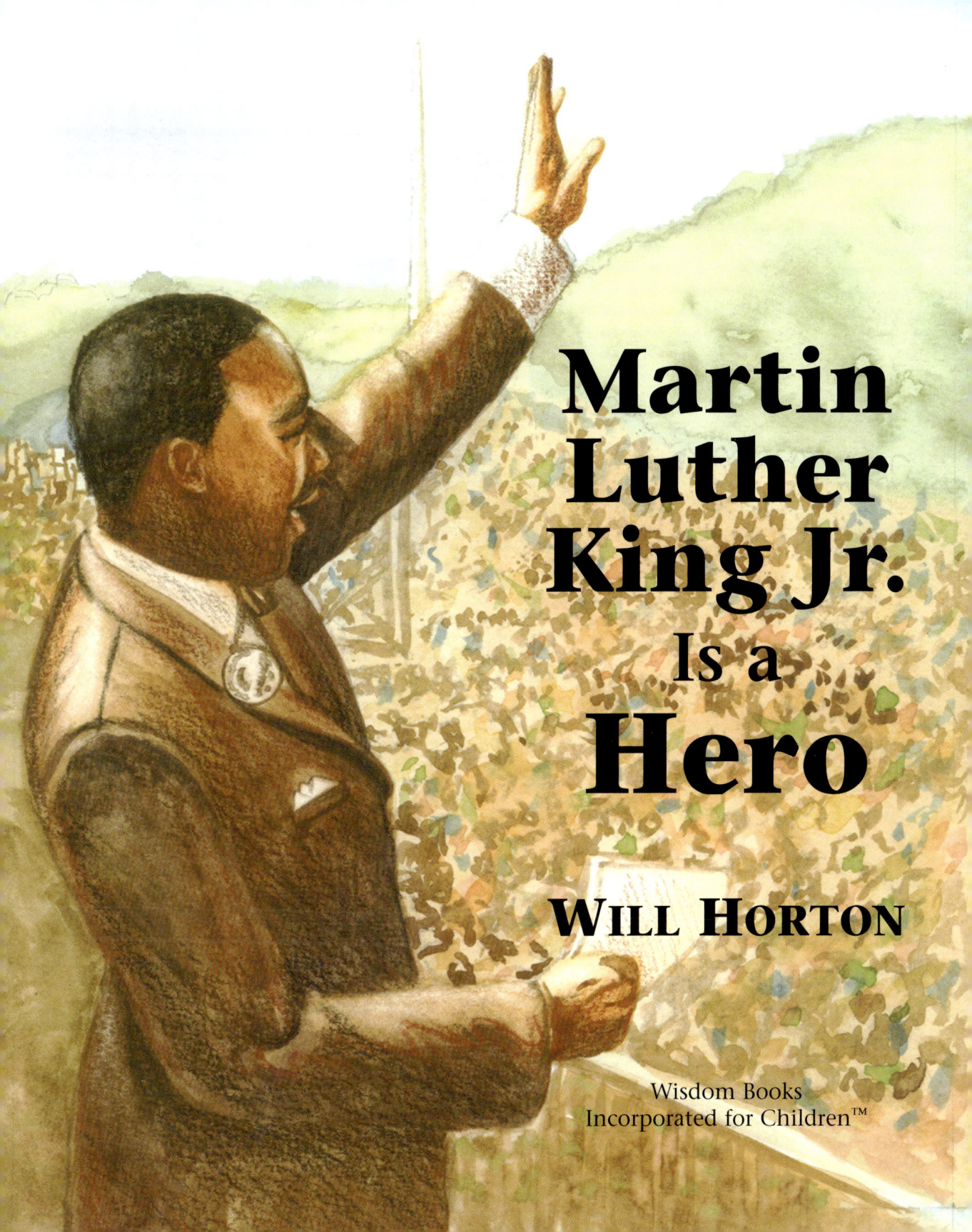

Wisdom Books Incorporated for Children™
An Imprint of Wisdom Books Incorporated
9029 South Western Avenue, Chicago, Illinois 60620

Copyright © 2007 by Will Horton
All rights reserved. No part of this book may be reproduced or transmitted in whole or part in any form electronically or mechanically, including photocopying, recording or by any information storage and retrieval system, without the written permission from the publisher or author. Wisdom Books Incorporated for Children is a trademark of Wisdom Books Incorporated.

Book design by Sans Serif
Printed in China

Summary: *Martin Luther King, Jr. Is a Hero* is an inspirational book for children. It includes a parent notes, vocabulary word list for beginning readers, and an author's note.

Library of Congress Cataloging-in-Publication Data
Horton, Will. Martin Luther King, Jr. Is a Hero
ISBN-13-: 978-1-892274-09-0
ISBN-10-: 1-892274-09-4

Library of Congress Control Number: 2006928070
1. King, Jr. Martin Luther, 2. Inspiration 3. Character 4. Life skills
5. African-American History 6. Racial tolerance 7. Civil rights 8. Children literature

www.wisdombooksinc.com

Parent Notes

Martin Luther King, Jr. Is a Hero is an inspirational book for children from early childhood—about 5 or 6 years of age, through middle and late childhood—approximately 12 years of age.

This book requires positive and interactive parenting, which includes recognizing the fact that parents are their children's first teachers and are active participants in their children's learning.

Positive parenting participation can have a profound influence on children's cognitive and intellectual development. Learning to read is one of the most important skills required for academic success and one of the key ingredients of children's successful cognitive and intellectual development. Readers become leaders in school and in life. Positive parenting influences contribute to a higher intelligence quotient (IQ) and academic achievement.

Promote Reading to Your Children

Read aloud to your children.

- Help your children learn word sound and sentence structure through reading.
- Promote language development and enhance reading readiness skills through reading aloud.
- Take your children to the library to explore different books.
- Get a library card for your children.
- Have your children read to you.
- Take your children to bookstore reading events.
- As your children become older encourage them to read at least 30 minutes each day.
- Help your children develop a joy of reading.
- Set yearly book reading goals for your children.

Discussion

As you read, identify keywords that your children may not know and discuss their meaning. Children's language skills develop more rapidly during middle and late childhood. When you introduce new words to children it will increase their language skills at an earlier development stage.

Discuss the meaning of the following words to facilitate comprehension and vocabulary development. You will find the grade level next to each keyword. Most children have the mental abilities to learn more than the school's standards and parent expectations. In fact, they have billions of neurons waiting for instructions.

Vocabulary Words for Beginning Readers

These are keywords used in this book and the grade level of the keyword. This information assists parents in the positive and interactive learning of their children.

- Another/K
- Arrest/3rd (The word *jail*/K many be substituted for *arrest*.)
- Best/K
- Dream/K
- Dreamer/K
- Example/2nd (The words *model*/3rd or *standard*/3rd may be substituted for *example*.)
- Freedom/K
- Friend/K
- Gift/K
- Goal/4th
- Great/K
- Greatness/1st
- Hero/K
- History/2nd

- Life/K
- Mind/K
- Mission/5th (The words *aim*/3rd, *ambition*/4th or *goal*/4th may be substituted for *mission*.)
- Peace/K
- Protest/4th (The word *object*/1st may be substituted for *protest*.)
- Success/K
- Threat/2nd
- Love/K
- Violence/2nd

Other Parent-Child Discussion Topics

- Discuss the civil rights movement with your children.
- Discuss the importance of the Civil Rights Act of 1964 and the Voting Rights Act of 1965.
- Discuss the role Martin Luther King, Jr. played in the success of the civil rights movement.
- Pick a word from the list above and have your children discuss the meaning with you.
- Discuss your children's goals.

Goals are objectives that parents and children set to work toward completing a definite purpose or mission. Goals help parents and children better plan their life's journey, aim and destination.

If you would like more information on the importance of setting goals and academic standards for children, you may check out my book, *Success Guideposts for African-American Children* from your local library, or e-mail me at www.willhorton.net. You can write me at Wisdom Books Incorporated, 9029 South Western Avenue, Chicago, Illinois 60620.

Lead nonviolent protests for justice and equality throug[h]

[Al]l labor has dignity. "A" average. Bachelor of Divinity [...]

December 1955 – Montgomery bus boycott

[Ph.]D. from Boston University   Devoted father an[d ...]

"I have a dream..."

"We shall overcome." 1963

"I just want to do God's will".

1964 – awar[d ...]

"I've been to the mo[untaintop ...]"

1977 – Medal of Honor

1986 – Birthday observe[d ...]

"...we as a people will get to the promised land".

"How long? Not long."

ut the nation

54, became pastor of Dexter Avenue Baptist Church.

ee.

1957 - SCLC is founded

1964 - signing of Civil Rights Act of 1964

usband

he March on Washington"

d the Nobel Peace Prize

taintop"

Martin Luther King, Jr. is a hero.

s a National Holiday

When I think of Martin Luther King, Jr.,
I think of the song "We Shall Overcome."

"We shall overcome, we shall overcome,
We shall overcome someday,
Oh, deep in my heart, I do believe,
We shall overcome someday."

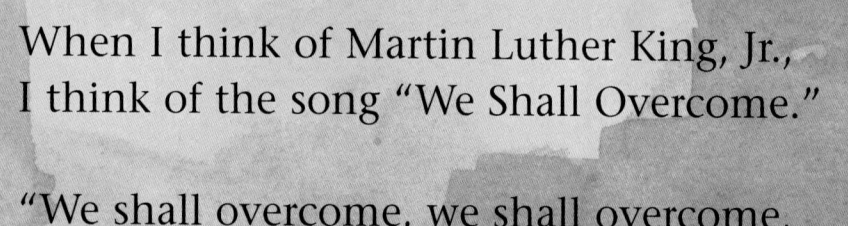

His mission was
 freedom, peace and love.
King wanted to help everyone
 to live their dreams.

Freedom was his call. King wanted to hear freedom ring, so that all young children could live their dreams.

Martin Luther King, Jr. is a hero.
Freedom was his goal.
He wanted freedom for all.

He continued to protest. There was always the threat of arrest.

He refused to quit.
Success was King's goal.

World News

THURSDAY, APRIL 4, 1968

MARTIN LUTHER KING IS ASSASSINATED IN MEMPHIS

Martin Luther King, Jr. gave you the greatest gifts you can give another person. He gave you love and his life.

THE REV. DR. MARTIN LUTHER KING Jr.

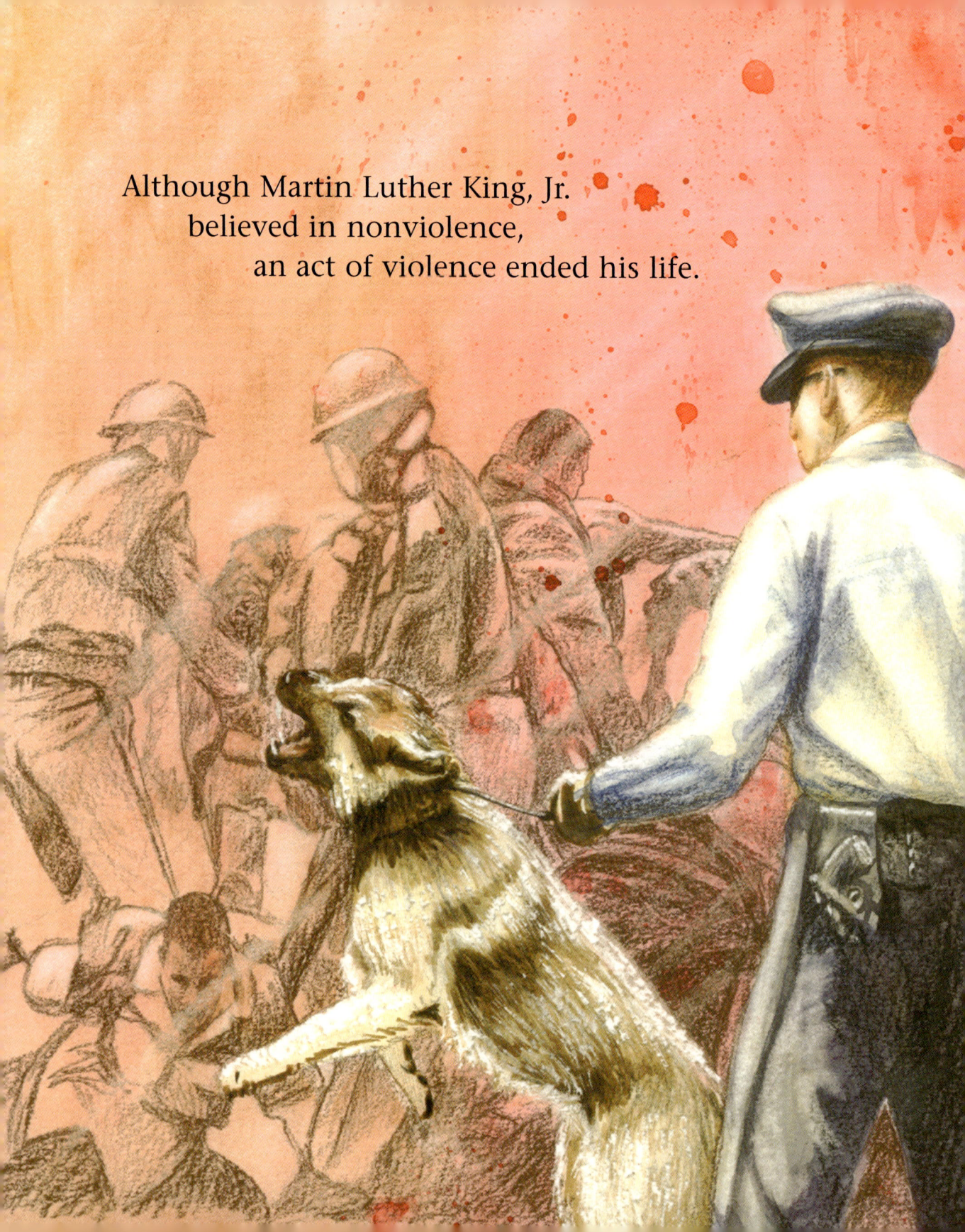

Although Martin Luther King, Jr. believed in nonviolence, an act of violence ended his life.

His life ended at age 39, but his life was great. King made the world a better place to live.

It matters not the length of your life,
but how you live your life.

What are you going to do to live your dreams, to become great?

When you give your best you can become great.

Martin Luther King, Jr. achieved his mission of freedom and equal rights.

Stay in school.

Make good grades.

Be the best that you can be.
  Use your mind to become great.

Let Martin Luther King Jr.'s life be an example for you to follow.

Learn to love and accept others that may not look like you.

Reach out and help somebody.

When you share your love
you will receive love.

Be kind to others.

Be a friend.

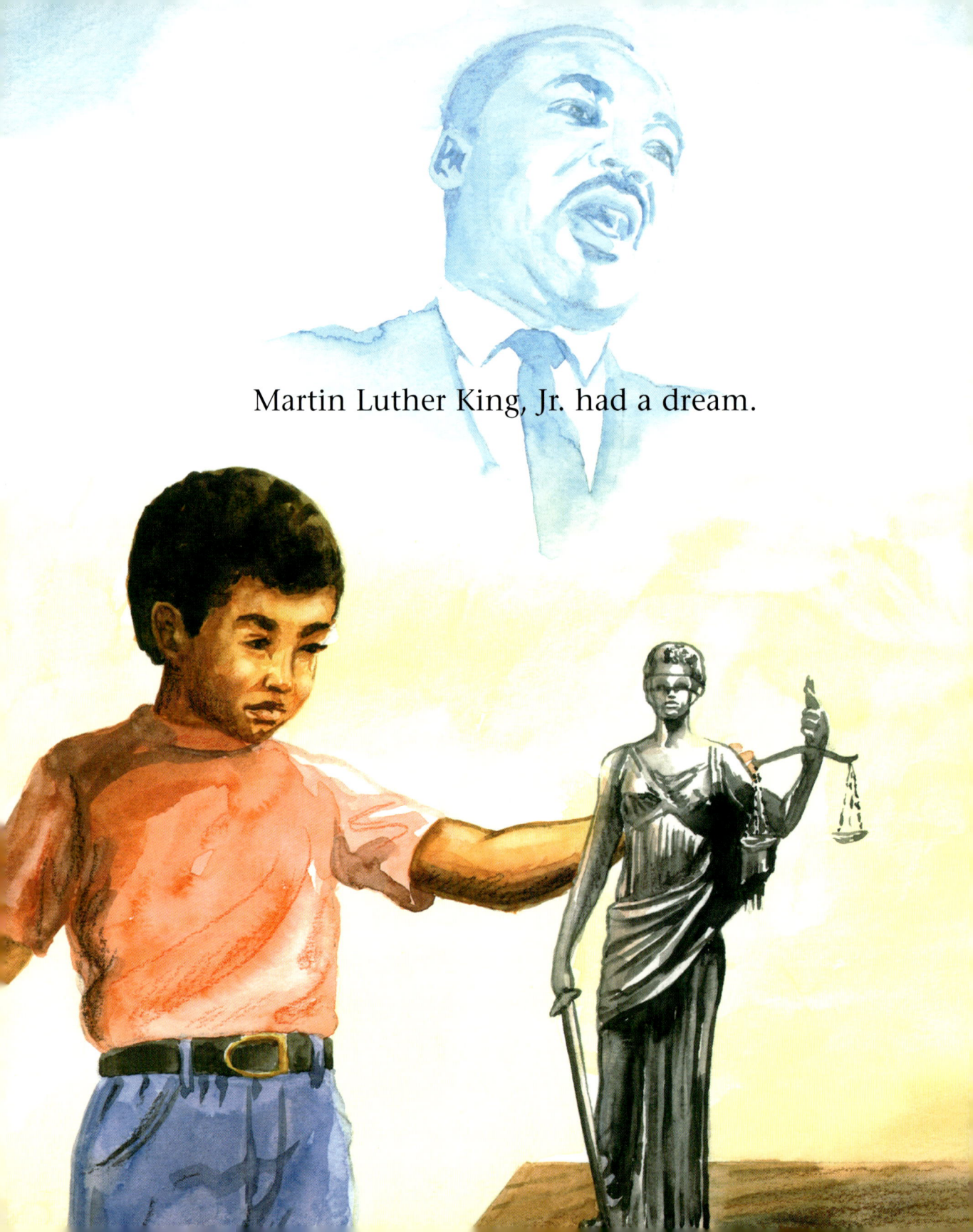

Martin Luther King, Jr. had a dream.

He dreamed of all the things
you could become in life.

King wanted you to live your dreams.

You can live your dreams,
if you believe you can.

You will find
 Martin Luther King, Jr.
  in the history books.

Martin Luther King, Jr. is a hero.

You can be like
Martin Luther King, Jr.,

if you discover your greatness.

FIRST PERSON ON MARS

You can become a hero.

And one day children will read about you in history books.

Martin Luther King, Jr. gave his love and life,
so you could spend your life living
the American Dream.

Martin Luther King, Jr. became great.

And so can you—
   if you set goals and work hard to achieve them.

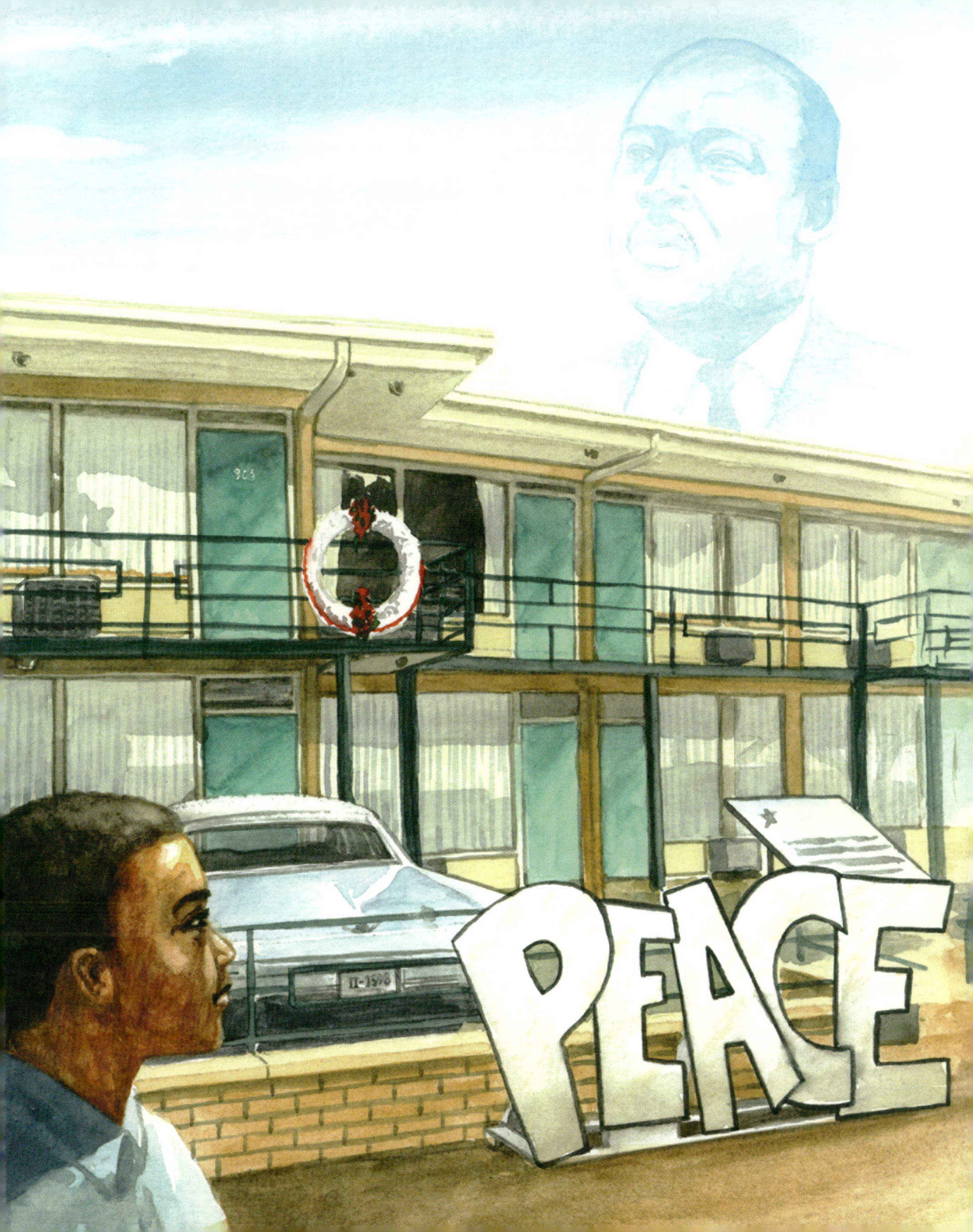
PEACE

Author's Note

Martin Luther King, Jr. was a Baptist minister, who was born in Atlanta, Georgia, on January 15, 1929. King became the leader of the civil rights movement and challenger to the injustice of segregation and racial discrimination in America during the 1950s and 1960s. King believed that the best way to defeat injustice was through nonviolent protest. "There is more power in socially organized masses on the march than there is in guns in the hands of a few desperate men," said King. He won the 1964 Nobel Peace Prize for his nonviolent philosophy and leadership in conducting courageous civil rights demonstrations.

Although, King campaigned against violence, he was often confronted and lived with threats and violence. King's life ended with an act of violence on April 4, 1968 when an assassin shot and killed him in Memphis, Tennessee during the Poor People's Campaign to support a strike by black garbage men. Although Martin Luther King, Jr.'s life ended at age 39, his life was sublime.

A hero is a person who has demonstrated distinguished courage, strength of character and noble qualities for his or her beliefs under difficult and challenging circumstances. Martin Luther King, Jr. met this criterion and is a hero. The word *hero* in this book denotes a man or woman. The word *heroine* can be introduced when your children understand the meaning of the word *heroine*.

Visit Will Horton's website at www.willhorton.net

About the Author

Will Horton is an educator and empowerment coach. He has over 20 years of educational experience from early childhood development to the college level. Horton is the author of *Success Guideposts for African-American Children: A Guide for Parents of Children Ages 0–18,* and *The 30 Power Principles: A Psychology of Success* and other books that are designed to teach proven principles and techniques to awaken and give life to your greatness.

Horton provides training programs and consulting in a variety of topics for parents, schools, government institutions and businesses.

Visit Will Horton's website at www.willhorton.net, or visit Wisdom Books Incorporated website at www.wisdombooksinc.com.

Mission Statement

Wisdom Books Incorporated for Children (WBIC)
> *To publish books that educate, inspire and empower children to give birth to their greatness.*